Speaking in Code

by Myka-Lynne Sokoloff

Scott Foresman
is an imprint of

Glenview, Illinois • Boston, Massachusetts • Chandler, Arizona
Upper Saddle River, New Jersey

Illustrators
6,7 Argosy; **9** David Harrington; **14** Steve Toole

Photographs
Every effort has been made to secure permission and provide appropriate credit for photographic material. The publisher deeply regrets any omission and pledges to correct errors called to its attention in subsequent editions.

Unless otherwise acknowledged, all photographs are the property of Pearson Education, Inc.

Photo locators denoted as follows: Top (T), Center (C), Bottom (B), Left (L), Right (R), Background (Bkgd)

CVR The Granger Collection, NY; **1** Bettmann/Corbis; **3** Pixtal/Punchstock; **5** Getty Images; **8** Getty Images; **10** Image copyright © The Metropolitan Museum of Art/Art Resource, NY; **11** The Granger Collection, NY; **12** © DK Images; **13** ©Bettmann/Corbis; **15** Sheila Terry/Photo Researchers, Inc.; **16** © Peter M. Fisher/Corbis.

ISBN 13: 978-0-328-51664-3
ISBN 10:   0-328-51664-3

2 3 4 5 6 7 8 9 10 V054 13 12 11 10

Cn U Rd Ths?

Do you ever use secret codes? When you send text or email messages, you may use special letters or symbols to stand for certain words. When you do this, you are using a code.

A code is a system of numbers, letters, or other symbols. Codes are used to send messages. Some codes are secret. Others, like Morse code, are known by many people. Morse code is one of the most important codes ever invented.

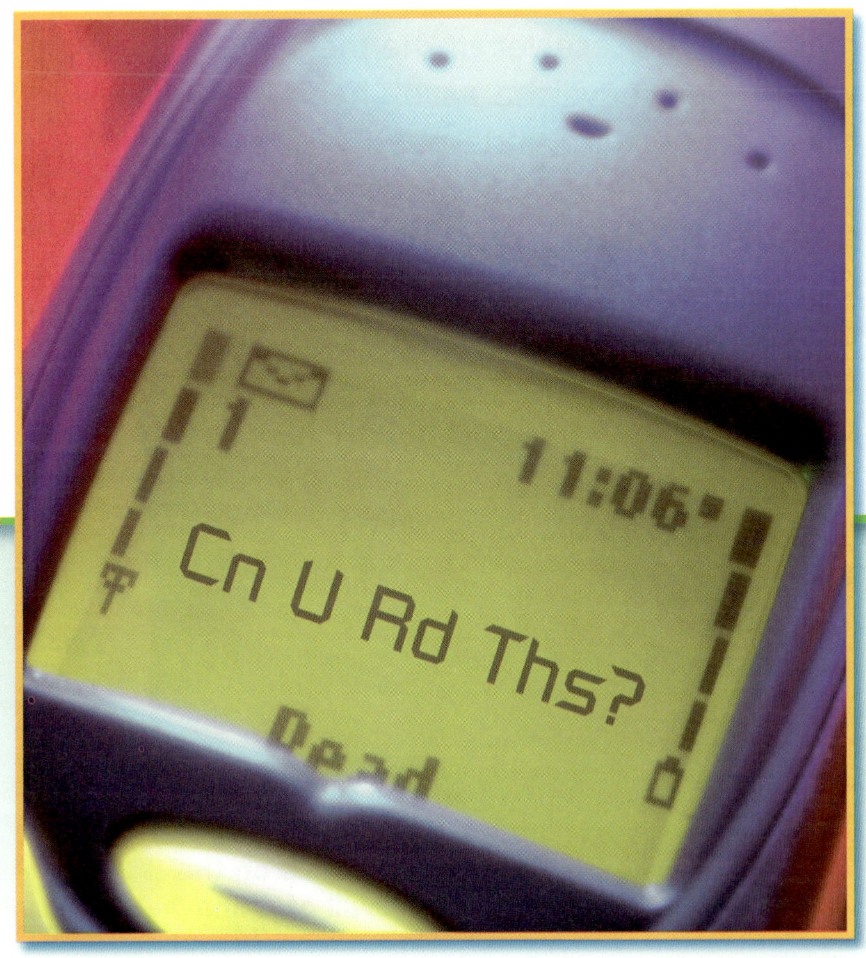

Codes in History

People have used codes throughout history to communicate secretly. In ancient Greece rulers sometimes sent messages by writing on the shaved heads of slaves. The ruler would wait for the slave's hair to grow back, and then send him far away on an exhausting trip to deliver the hidden message. The receiver of the message would then shave the slave's head to reveal the writing underneath.

Today ancient signal towers still stand on parts of the Great Wall of China. These towers were once used to send smoke signals. Puffs of smoke communicated simple messages. These smoke signals were used mostly in times of war.

Signal towers on the Great Wall of China

**Semaphore

Semaphore (SEM-uh-for) code was developed in France around 1800. It uses two flags. Each flag is divided into two colored triangles. The flags are held a certain way to signal each letter of the alphabet. The sender moves the flags to spell out words.

Dozens of semaphore stations carried messages throughout France during Napoleon Bonaparte's time. Napoleon used this system to send and receive messages from his headquarters during battle.

This is the code for "Help."

The Telegraph

People who wanted to send more detailed messages could not use codes like semaphore and smoke signals. It also was impossible to use these systems to send messages quickly over great distances.

Some inventors thought that the new and exciting power of electricity could be used to send messages. In the 1700s, people did not know much about electricity. They did not use it as we do today, but scientists were beginning to understand more about it. Inventors believed that electricity was the key to sending long distance messages, but they weren't sure how it could be done.

Electricity causes the lightning we see in the sky.

At first, attempts to use electricity to send messages were unsuccessful. A man named Don Francisco Salva y Campillo had a plan to link electrical wires to people. Each person would be assigned a letter of the alphabet. He would then send an electrical current through the wire to signal a letter. The person connected to that wire would get an intense shock and call out his or her assigned letter. Now that's a shocking idea!

By the 1830s inventors on both sides of the Atlantic were trying to make telegraph machines, or machines that send and receive messages. One such inventor was Samuel Morse. He first became interested in electricity in college, but he did not know that much about science. At the time he wasn't a scientist but a portrait painter.

Painting by S. F. B. Morse of his daughter Susan

Samuel Morse

Morse found two partners to help with his invention. Leonard Gale helped Morse design a telegraph system. The 1837 system used an on-and-off key to send electrical signals along a wire. Long and short signals, or taps on the key, appeared as dashes and dots at the other end of the wire. The signals made sounds that could be heard at the other end too.

Morse's other partner was Alfred Vail. In 1838 Vail suggested using these dashes and dots as a code. Each letter of the alphabet would be represented by a set of long and short signals.

Long signals (dashes) are read aloud as *dah*. Short signals (dots) are pronounced *dit*. The system worked so well that some people receiving Morse code could understand up to seventy-five words per minute!

Morse Code

A	. —	J	. — — —
B	— . . .	K	— . —
C	— . — .	L	. — . .
D	— . .	M	— —
E	.	N	— .
F	. . — .	O	— — —
G	— — .	P	. — — .
H	. . . .	Q	— — . —
I	. .	R	. — .

An early telegraph

S	. . .	2	. . _ _ _
T	_	3	. . . _ _
U	. . _	4	. . . . _
V	. . . _	5	. . . . .
W	. _ _	6	_ . . . .
X	_ . . _	7	_ _ . . .
Y	_ . _ _	8	_ _ _ . .
Z	_ _ . .	9	_ _ _ _ .
1	. _ _ _ _	0	_ _ _ _ _

Effects of the Telegraph

The United States was growing rapidly in the mid-1800s. Before the telegraph, the Pony Express, with its skilled riders, was the fastest way to send messages. But even they took several days to cross the country. The telegraph made it possible to send and receive messages quickly across the country.

Around the same time, railroads began to cross the country as well. Before the telegraph, railroad workers couldn't tell in advance whether a track was clear. As a result there were many accidents on the tracks. Railroads became safer with the telegraph system in place.

The telegraph helped people in other ways too. Businesses sent messages about products, prices, and shipments. Newspapers could receive news from far away. Suddenly many people began to read a daily newspaper. Better communication and transportation made the world seem smaller.

Each red dot indicates a telegraph office in the 1840s.

Telegraph to Telephone and More

For about thirty years, using the telegraph to send Morse code was the fastest way to send messages. However, a man named Alexander Graham Bell had an idea for a better telegraph machine. Bell noticed he could hear sounds over the wire. He began to work on a new invention that would send speech over the electrical wires . . . and it worked! Bell placed the first telephone call in 1876.

Alexander Graham Bell

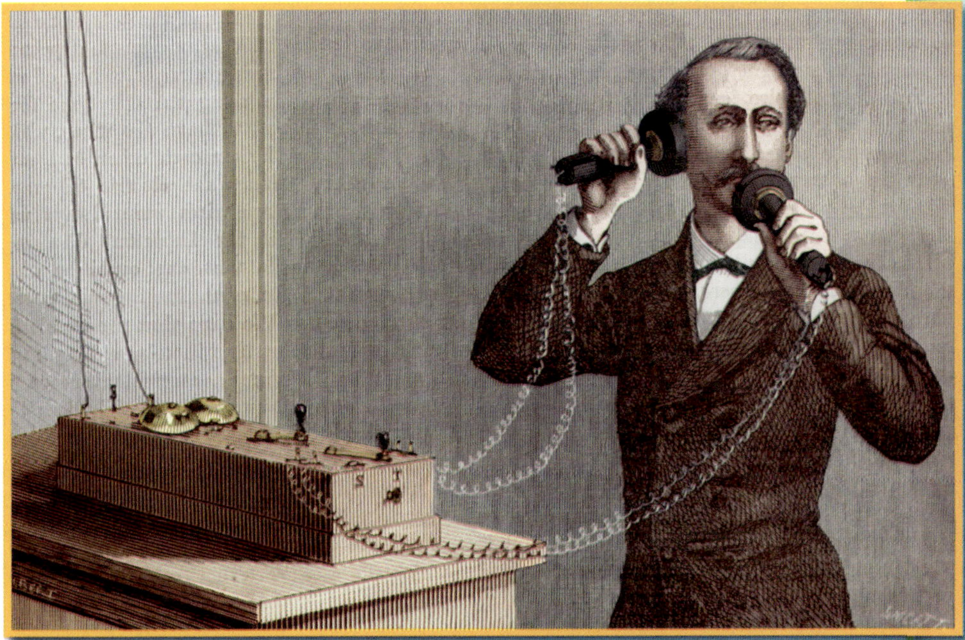

Hello, Operator!

For many years, long distance phone calls were very expensive, so people did not make them too often. Instead, people sent important messages by telegram. The message was printed at a telegraph office and delivered by hand. Some people even sent singing telegrams.

The word *telegraph* means any machine that sends or receives messages over long distances. So when you send an email or a text message, you are actually a telegraph operator too.

An early telegraph

S . . .
T _
U . . _
V . . . _
W . _ _
X _ . . _
Y _ . _ _
Z _ _ . .
1 . _ _ _ _

2 . . _ _ _
3 . . . _ _
4 . . . . _
5 . . . . .
6 _ . . . .
7 _ _ . . .
8 _ _ _ . .
9 _ _ _ _ .
0 _ _ _ _ _

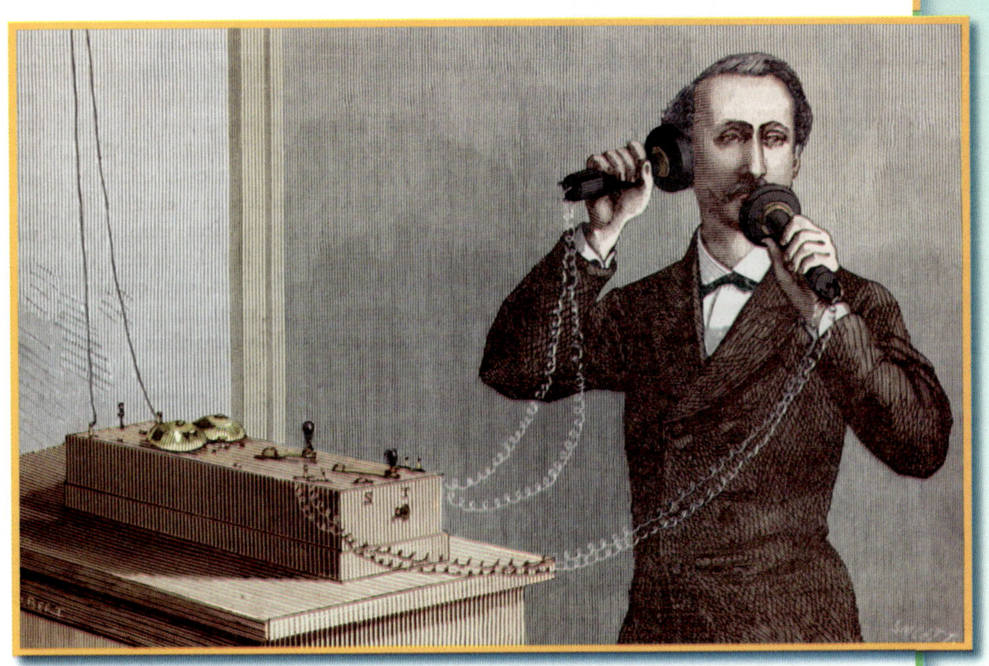

Morse's other partner was Alfred Vail. In 1838 Vail suggested using these dashes and dots as a code. Each letter of the alphabet would be represented by a set of long and short signals.

Long signals (dashes) are read aloud as *dah*. Short signals (dots) are pronounced *dit*. The system worked so well that some people receiving Morse code could understand up to seventy-five words per minute!

Morse Code

A . −
B − . . .
C − . − .
D − . .
E .
F . . − .
G − − .
H . . . .
I . .

J . − − −
K − . −
L . − . .
M − −
N − .
O − − −
P . − − .
Q − − . −
R . − .

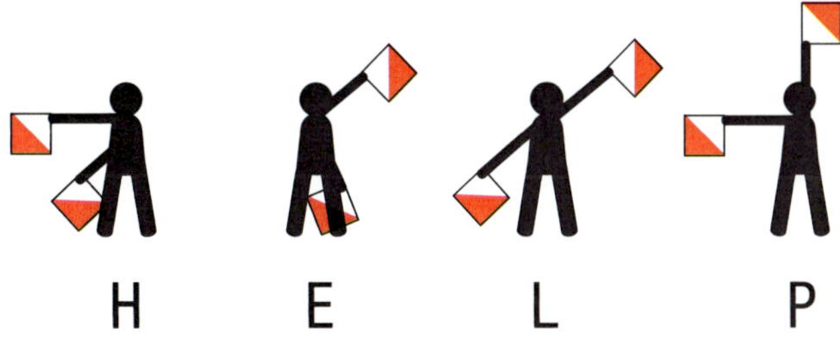

Illustrators
6,7 Argosy; **9** David Harrington; **14** Steve Toole

Photographs
Every effort has been made to secure permission and provide appropriate credit for photographic material. The publisher deeply regrets any omission and pledges to correct errors called to its attention in subsequent editions.

Unless otherwise acknowledged, all photographs are the property of Pearson Education, Inc.

Photo locators denoted as follows: Top (T), Center (C), Bottom (B), Left (L), Right (R), Background (Bkgd)

CVR The Granger Collection, NY; **1** Bettmann/Corbis; **3** Pixtal/Punchstock; **5** Getty Images; **8** Getty Images; **10** Image copyright © The Metropolitan Museum of Art/Art Resource, NY; **11** The Granger Collection, NY; **12** © DK Images; **13** ©Bettmann/Corbis; **15** Sheila Terry/Photo Researchers, Inc.; **16** © Peter M. Fisher/Corbis.

ISBN 13: 978-0-328-51664-3
ISBN 10:   0-328-51664-3